NATIONAL PARKS
AND THE
COUNTRYSIDE

NATIONAL PARKS
AND THE
COUNTRYSIDE

BY

SIR NORMAN BIRKETT

Chairman of The Standing Committee on National Parks, & President of the Friends of The Lake District

THE REDE LECTURE

1945

CAMBRIDGE

AT THE UNIVERSITY PRESS

1945

CAMBRIDGE
UNIVERSITY PRESS

University Printing House, Cambridge CB2 8BS, United Kingdom

Published in the United States of America by Cambridge University Press, New York

Cambridge University Press is part of the University of Cambridge.

It furthers the University's mission by disseminating knowledge in the pursuit of education, learning and research at the highest international levels of excellence.

www.cambridge.org
Information on this title: www.cambridge.org/9781107674776

First published 1945
Re-issued 2014

A catalogue record for this publication is available from the British Library

ISBN 978-1-107-67477-6 Paperback

NATIONAL PARKS & THE COUNTRYSIDE

IT IS ALMOST FORTY YEARS SINCE I STOOD IN this place to compete for the Winchester Reading Prize.

Those years, sometimes long and laborious, now seem to have gone with bewildering swiftness, but some of the emotions of that memorable day remain. I still recall the warm satisfaction which came from the knowledge that it was to be given me in that hour what I should say—a most admirable and humane procedure, as it seems to me now at this moment of reappearance.

And if the intervening years have given much, they have also taken much away; not the least of their takings being the unbelievably confident young man of that far-distant occasion. To-day I am as conscious of my obvious shortcomings as, according to Lord Bowen, His Majesty's Judges are conscious of each other's; and I am most deeply sensible of the great honour it is to stand where so many distinguished men have stood before me in accordance with the ancient endowment of Sir Robert Rede. And if so great a man as A. E. Housman could say of those who selected him to be the Leslie Stephen lecturer, that he condemned their judgment and deplored their choice, I, at least, standing afar off, and not daring so much as to lift my eyes, may justly and feelingly echo it.

I cannot make the claim to any special knowledge of my own that Kinglake so engagingly made in the Preface to *Eöthen*; rather do I know the painful sharpness of the truth proclaimed by Stevenson that 'neither clearness, compression, nor beauty of language come to any living creature, till after a busy and prolonged acquaintance with the subject on hand'. Yet despite all this, I count myself fortunate in being allowed to choose the subject of National Parks and the Countryside at this particular time. I do not think that choice will cause any undue perturbation to the watching shade of Sir Robert Rede.

A little tolerance is no doubt needed to bring it within the sphere of 'humanity, logic, or philosophy', and though it may lack the quality of high excitement to which the age is now accustomed, it is perhaps none the worse for that. There has been no lack of excitement in one form or another during the past six years, and when the absorbing task of beating the sword into the ploughshare, or, more properly, the tank into the tractor, is producing excitements, and more than excitements, of which the prophet Micah could have known little, it is perhaps a good thing to compose ourselves for a little time under our own vine and fig tree, and to contemplate the quiet of the countryside and the place of national parks.

After all, and with all false sentiment laid aside, we do well to remember that it was some glimpse of the countryside as an essential part of what is vaguely called 'The English Tradition' that many men held before them during six years of war, and it was with some picture of that same countryside before them that many of them died.

'This precious stone set in the silver sea' was certainly never on their lips, nor consciously in their minds, but some familiar and well-loved spot was with them as a strength and stay in many moments of their hard experience. And whilst it is, no doubt, the highest wisdom to keep a sense of proportion in all things, and to avoid making claims of the extravagant and fantastic kind, it is simply the plainest of plain truths to say that the countryside has a supreme contribution to make to the national life at this particular moment of our history, although the nature and the quality of that contribution is yet but imperfectly apprehended:

> Beauty crieth in an attic and no man regardeth:
> O God! O Montreal!

The creation of national parks is, in some measure, bound up with the claim of the countryside to contribute to the full and harmonious national life. I say 'in some measure', for it is not suggested that the establishment of national parks will solve the problems of the countryside. Those problems are very real and complicated and highly controversial, and it is of the first importance to appreciate the limits of the claim made on behalf of national parks.

One of the most distinguished of our writers on the countryside has recently (and somewhat unkindly) said in his most attractive autobiography that 'the creation of national parks is discussed with much parade and much ignorance'. I should count myself fortunate to be acquitted on this indictment, but if convicted, would desire to plead in mitigation the precise nature of the claims made. The creation of national parks is only a part, though a most important and valuable part, of the much greater work of preserving the whole countryside. The detachment of that part from the larger scene, and the formulation and presentation of the separate and complete proposals for national parks is a comparatively late development in the history of preservation, and has come about quite naturally as experience has shown its wisdom.

National parks are a distinguishable and determinate part of the much larger problem of controlling the use of land, and growing experience has shown it to be most desirable that they should be kept apart from the more general needs of land planning as a whole. National parks can be created now without injury to any other cause or interest; they compete with no other 'social' need of the day, but aid and supplement those needs, and are in themselves a 'social' need of the highest possible kind.

If the work of preservation on a national scale is to wait until a complete national policy is fashioned and formulated, until final decisions are made on all the highly controversial questions, it may very well be that some of the most beautiful areas in the land will pass beyond the reach of any salvation.

The great need is to make a sound national beginning, and to make it now by the creation of national parks, so that they may serve as a guide and stimulus and encouragement in that work of preservation which is the professed aim of Governments and people alike. When national parks are established, some, at least, of the growing dangers to the countryside will be overcome, the fairest places still left in these islands will be secure from all assault arising either from accident or design, and a very great contribution indeed will have been made to the happiness of millions in town and country alike.

It must always be a matter for surprise that no such step has yet been taken in this country, particularly when it is remembered, as Mr Belloc has reminded us, that 'the love of England has in it the love of landscape, as has the love of no other country'. For six centuries the poets have sung the beauties of the country, and their songs, or fragments of them, have gone eternally into the common speech. For all the coloured counties, and for all the changing seasons, for the magnificent and awe-inspiring, as well as for the meanest flower that blows, there is high and satisfying expression.

The great novelists have set down the country scene upon the living page and dressed it with a kind of immortality. The social historians have recorded the events that changed the face of the countryside throughout the centuries, adding a new beauty of their own, the beauty of association. And the essayists and diarists, geologists and botanists, bird and animal lovers, fishermen and country parsons, praisers and glorifiers of every kind have made up that exceeding great army which no man can number.

The countryside is commonly spoken of as a great national heritage, and so it is; but the literature of the countryside is a most noble heritage too, and of a range and power and beauty quite without equal. All the great names are there, and some of the very greatest, it is good to think, are in a very special sense the possession of this University. Herrick is ours, no less surely than Milton or Spenser. But the very greatest, down to the most lowly, give full and dutiful expression to that love of the countryside which is a national characteristic.

And with all this, there are still no national parks! That wilderness of beauty the poets immortalized has become too often the wilderness of mean streets, the glory departed, and all the magic gone as though it had never been. In recent years, the beauty of the countryside has been destroyed on a very great scale, and that loss is now irremediable.

The work of preservation has always been hard, and at times a little thankless, but latterly it has become quite heart-breaking. To save a footpath or a lonely moor or a piece of common land from destruction, or to preserve some historic and beautiful spot, the voluntary societies, established for this purpose, have had to toil and sweat, to cajole and implore, to plead and beseech, lead deputations to Ministers, waylay Members of Parliament, write letters to *The Times* and *The Manchester Guardian*, raise Defence Funds, and, in sheer desperation, employ counsel. And for all the comfort that the 'severe and sour-complexioned' men in Government departments (as Izaak Walton would have called them, and as they inevitably seem to be at such moments) can give, Wordsworth might never have written a line, 'Tintern Abbey' which Sir William Beach Thomas believes to contain the whole creed of the countryman, 'to be repeated aloud in places of beauty where altars are lifted to the north and south and east and west, and wherever the eyes are bent', might be quite without meaning, and that exceeding great army might never have been mobilized. Not that Government departments must be blamed too much. The burden lies heavily upon us all, and the blame must be much more widely distributed.

As things are at present, and as we have for so long allowed them to be, the harassed Minister and his advisers have a score of conflicting claims to harmonize, all put forward with zeal, and some with discretion.

The great city needs water, and water it must by all means have. The claims of the beauty lovers in the catchment areas, fearful of the impounding of lakes and tarns and rivers, with knowledge, maybe, of Thirlmere and Haweswater as they once were, no doubt seem at times to be a little remote from stern reality; and certainly, it may be conceded, the thirst of the body is more readily understandable than that divine thirst which from the soul doth rise. The country areas need electricity both for light and power, and overhead pylons seem to be a most regrettable necessity; but the indignant deputation to the Minister wrings its hands and speaks like Gordon Bottomley 'To an Ironmaster'.

On the one side are those who wish to 'develop' the land, as the official phrasing goes, those who wish to quarry and to mine with the almost unavoidable consequence of unsightly slag heaps and polluted and disfigured becks, those who wish to plaster the lovely and austere hills with ugly, monotonous conifer plantations, those who wish to drive great roads in the most unsuitable places, those who wish to take some remote and tranquil spot and use it for military purposes; and on the other side are those who wish to meet national needs in a practical way, but believe that this can be done without too much sacrifice of native beauty.

What, therefore, is the unhappy and tortured Minister to do? When the deputation, at long last, withdraws, he removes the expression of intense and sympathetic interest from his features, and turns, no doubt, to Hardy or Gilbert White for consolation, but all that he has permitted himself to say is that he is most grateful to the deputation, and the matter will have his most careful and earnest attention. Now the establishment of national parks will change all that for some at least of the most beautiful and precious parts of the land.

A discussion or exposition of what I may call the machinery of national parks would be out of place here, but it has become quite clear that an indispensable element in any scheme of national planning is the setting up of one single authority for all national park areas. A National Parks Commission must be created, specially appointed and directed by Act of Parliament, administering a special

National Parks Fund under parliamentary control, with a continuity of policy and power unaffected by the chances and changes of political life. The choice of areas for national parks, the definition of the boundaries, the nature and extent of every kind of development within the national park boundaries—all these matters would be in the hands of the Commissioners, who would be appointed by the Minister of Town and Country Planning, and the Minister would be answerable for the Commissioners in Parliament. The creation of such a Commission is regarded as quite fundamental, and it is apparent that the Government departments themselves would be very great gainers.

The establishment of national parks can only come about, of course, by the act of the Government; but the chief reason why national parks have not yet been created is the lack of the right kind of public opinion. The countryside is highly prized, but it is not thought to be in any real danger. There is still so much of it, and despite the dismal prophecies, it still survives. The larger grievous loss is not seen, and year by year the steady remorseless destruction continues. It is now nearly twenty years ago since the spokesmen of the National Trust when giving evidence before the Addison Committee said:

> ...in the most characteristic part of England, natural beauty is disappearing at an alarming rate. The ordinary country which has been the pride of our poets and painters, and indeed of the whole English people for

centuries is being every year more and more rapidly destroyed or disfigured beyond recognition. The nation itself, which through its chief spokesmen is always deploring these irremediable losses, is itself by its public action one of their chief causes.

National parks, in the highest sense, are a popular cause with a place in the public imagination, and supported by an instructed public opinion. But that public opinion needs to grow in volume and knowledge and power. The idea is much too common that national parks are formal and controlled and 'faddy', and the talk of natural beauty still rouses too much suspicion in the robust-minded; it is still thought that there is to be some extensive and needless prohibition, some vast and unnecessarily loud 'Stop it'.

And there are so many reforms that seem more immediately urgent, affecting this difficult business of living more closely and intimately. Some reforms, long desired and awaited, come in unexpected moments because of the inexorable pressure of great events. It was said that it needed a great European war to bring about Daylight Saving! But national parks can never hope for help of this kind; indeed, sometimes the very stars in their courses seem to fight against them.

In times of great national emergency, when all activity is concentrated on high national purposes, the claims of national parks cannot get a hearing; and when the emergency is happily past, the nation turns to other problems the emergency has left, and national parks are again forgotten.

In the past, nobody has cared quite enough to undertake the hard and somewhat dreary task of making a national plan as a matter of high policy, with all the multifarious and multitudinous details carefully worked out; and so the tragedy has continued down to our day, the towns spreading into the country in the most haphazard way, beauty spots being transformed into places of horror, and the whole countryside down to the very coasts littered with shanties and bungalows, shacks and notice boards, and all that is squalid and disfiguring.

Now the present moment in our national affairs is charged with the highest promise for national parks; it is the most hopeful moment in their history, and that is why I count it a great privilege to speak of them in this place to-day. This is supremely the moment when the claims of national parks can be advanced with great confidence and surety. After the experiences of the past six years it is inevitable and altogether praiseworthy that there should be a great stirring in men's minds, a vast quickening of man's social conscience. And even if it were thought that this is put too high, it is at least inevitable that after so much sacrifice and suffering so nobly borne, it should be felt that some compensation might be found for so large a calamity, that something nobler should emerge for those who had endured so much, that there should be in the somewhat wistful phrase—a better world.

At the time of the Great Plague, the Bishop of Rochester spoke of the greatness of heart with which the obscure multitude of London had borne their calamities, as one of the most honourable events that ever happened. In our day, we have seen humble folk everywhere put on courage like a garment. So it is that side by side with the determination to destroy the evil things of the world, there has sprung up the desire to fulfil the social needs, to spread education, to build the houses, to provide employment, to give security, and to establish a better mode of life, with opportunities for the right use of leisure, and a more gracious way of living.

It is here that national parks make their very highest claim. When more than a century ago Wordsworth put forward his great claim for the preservation of the Lake District, he also took the very highest ground. He said of that delectable spot that it must be protected from rash assault because it was 'capable of satisfying the most intense cravings for the tranquil, the lovely, and the perfect to which man, the noblest of her creatures, is subject'.

Some years ago, the present Master of Trinity made an appeal for national parks on the same high grounds, as a fulfilment of the deepest needs of men. He said:

It is a question of spiritual values. Without vision the people perish, and without sight of the beauty of nature the spiritual power of the British people will be atrophied....

By the side of religion, by the side of Science, by the side of Poetry and Art stands natural beauty, not as a rival to these, but as the common inspirer and nourisher of them all, and with a secret of her own beside....

In that fairer and better world on which the hopes and desires of millions are set, national parks must have their honoured and useful place, making the contribution they are so well able to make to the happiness and well-being of this generation, and of the generations still to come.

Now having made these great and distinctive claims for national parks it might be well to try to say what they are, and what is perhaps of equal importance, what they are not; for much misconception exists. The name itself is troublesome, for it needs explanation, a fatal fault. But it cannot now be altered, and it is difficult to think of a satisfactory substitute.

Many people still think of national parks as being in some obscure way connected with the great parks they have known in various parts of the country surrounding some old mansion, but now, by state action, made accessible to the people at large. The thoughts of some fly to St James's Park or to Windsor Great Park, or the parks provided by local authorities in the great cities. Some, no doubt, think of asphalt paths and trim gardens, where 'tulips bloom as they are told', and where forbidding notices and uniformed keepers abound. Some, again, think of national parks as being purely 'nature reserves' where the wild life of both plants and animals is protected and sheltered; some as though they were the green belts cast around the circumference of spreading cities; and some as though they were a kind of 'Forest Park' where waste land not useable for the production of state timber is made available for public access. But the most widespread and the most natural misconception is that national parks are areas of wild natural beauty modelled on the great national parks of Canada and the United States of America. It must be plainly stated that none of these things, however admirable they may be in themselves, can ever be substitutes for true national parks in this country.

No doubt there will be nature reserves inside the national park areas, and the care of plant and animal life will be a consideration always to be kept in mind. Indeed, in recent years, many writers have pointed out the fact that the native vegetation is an essential element in natural beauty, and should be deliberately conserved. There is a passage in one of the books of that indefatigable friend of all out-door societies and national parks—the Rev. H. H. Symonds—that I must give myself the pleasure of quoting in this connexion:

> On the way up you pass lovely tarns and marsh grasses —there is surely no grass so beautiful as the marsh grasses —and stonecrops and saxifrages, if it is not too late in August. There is some soft, boggy ground by such pools: but are they not worth the softness? For all bog has its own virtues, and the best of all are those vegetable consolations which abound on it. There is that emerald green of the moss which floats on water-holes to trap the ingenuous. And Sphagnum moss (is it still dried to stop bleeding?) with long water-sodden stems and curiously varied colour in its foliage—green, yellow, pink, red.
>
> There is the charmingly exotic sundew—deep crimson petals and sweet sticky traps of hair, which entertain the

passing fly only to digest him. The greenish-yellow rosette of the butterwort, imitating the star-fish; bog myrtle with its resinous scent and spring catkins; the bog asphodel and its splendid little red pokers; grass of Parnassus, a star for brightness, and silk for texture; and last, and best, fields of the cotton grass, nodding its lovely head among the pinks and browns of the bog grasses by some upland pool.

What a catalogue of refreshment and beauty.

But national parks are much more than nature reserves or forest parks or green belts. They are the regions of our finest landscape made national possessions by the deliberate choice of the nation, whatever their precise locality, preserved by the nation in their natural beauty, made accessible to the people, and particularly to cross-country walkers, and brought into the fullest public service consistent with these ends. Behind that simple and perhaps over-simplified statement lie problems of great complexity of which experience has taught me not to be unmindful. The statement itself needs some expansion and embellishment which by your kindness I will attempt before I sit down; but the main moving idea of national parks is there—regions of great natural beauty, fully used for the purposes for which they are best fitted, and for adventure, health, recreation and happiness.

It is clear at once that there can be no thought of attempting to rival the great national parks of America and Canada. When I first had the pleasure of visiting the great Canadian national park at Banff, and was in the midst of a long and somewhat solitary walk in what seemed to me to be quite unexplored country, I well remember the alarm with which I heard a small boy, whom I encountered, say with great unconcern—'You'll meet a couple of bears a little farther on'. That, at least, can't happen here. So long ago as 1885 the Government of Canada set aside this area of ten square miles in Alberta around the hot mineral springs of Banff as a great national park, and to-day Canada has seventeen such areas covering no less than 29,000 square miles. This is exactly one-half of the total area of England and Wales. These national parks of Canada contain almost every kind of scenery—mountains, hills, rivers, lakes, islands, the sea coast, forests and woodlands—and provide for riding, walking, motoring, camping, bathing, canoeing, ski-ing, and every conceivable kind of outdoor recreation. Happy, happy Canada to be so favoured; but the mere recital forbids all thought of emulation or rivalry.

In 1832 the United States of America set aside 'Hot Springs' in Arkansas as a great national park, and in 1872 added the famous Yellowstone Park as a 'pleasure ground for the enjoyment and benefit of the people'. In 1916 the national park service of America was instituted to serve 'those areas of unusual scenic beauty...set aside by Congress to conserve the scenery and the natural and historic objects and the wild life therein, and to provide for the enjoyment of the same in such manner and by such means as will leave them unimpaired for the enjoyment of future generations'. The national parks of America cover vast areas, and are now regarded as essential to the well-being of the people, but, as with Canada, we cannot compete, we can but envy, admire, and learn.

For myself I find it easy to obey Bunyan's Mr Great-Heart in this matter, and to hearken to what the shepherd's boy saith, for here, at least,

> I am content with what I have,
> Little be it, or much.

Here we are quite without any 'virgin' country; for good or ill, the hand of man is on all things.

But if grandeur in the American sense be lacking, there is yet to be found something that can be found nowhere else in the world—that rare and almost inexpressible charm springing from the long association of the land with the hopes and desires and purposes of the people throughout their notable history. No country in the world of anything like the same size is so rich in the possession of natural beauty linked with historic interest, and no countryside in the world has ever compelled such devotion, or indeed, adoration.

In that book which Mr Wells regards as his happiest book, and which I think is the best of all his books—*The History of Mr Polly*—there are a few sentences which express this feeling for the countryside in the most beautiful and effective way:

> There is no countryside like the English countryside for those who have learned to love it; its firm yet gentle lines of hill and dale, its ordered confusion of features, its deer-parks and downland, its castles and stately houses, its

hamlets and old churches, its farms and ricks and great barns and ancient trees, its pools and ponds and shining threads of rivers, its flower-starred hedgerows, its orchards and woodland patches, its village greens and kindly Inns. Other countrysides have their pleasant aspects, but none such variety, none that shine so steadfastly throughout the year...none that change scene and character in three miles of walking, nor have so mellow a sunlight, nor so diversified a cloudland, nor confess the perpetual refreshment of the strong soft winds that blow from off the sea, as our mother England does.

This then is the nature and quality of that countryside from which the national parks are to be formed.

Almost of necessity, the larger parts of the national park areas will be in mountain or upland country, particularly where such native wildness as we still possess, remains; but the grander stretches of wild coast-line make an insistent call for preservation; and the sea equally with the land is an essential part of English life. As Stevenson said: 'The sea is our approach and bulwark; it has been the scene of our greatest triumphs and dangers; and we are accustomed in lyrical strains to claim it as our own'. That coast-line is in very deadly danger, for 'our coast changes almost from week to week: cliffs fall, capes push seaward, or drift at the tide's pluck like the shadow on a dial'. But by far the worst injury to the coast comes not from nature but from man. 'The hinterland of the beaches plague-spotted by shacks', in the language of Sir William Beach Thomas, is the dreadful price already exacted for delay and inaction.

Of the 58,000 square miles in England and Wales, the land which can properly be set aside for national parks is necessarily limited. Some of the most beautiful areas are too small to be dealt with nationally, or are already being used for afforestation or some other purpose. But when full allowance is made for existing uses, and possible future uses of the land, the needs of agriculture, the demands of industry, and every other national necessity, it is estimated that 6000 square miles should and could with advantage be devoted to national parks. This would permit of twenty separate areas of some 300 square miles each; and no national park, except for very special reasons, should be less than 200 square miles in extent.

It is not contemplated that all these national parks should be established at once; but it is most desirable that at least half a dozen should be created the moment the war ends, and that three or more should be added each year until all the available land is included, protection being given to them in the meantime. The choice of the first half-dozen national parks need occasion no difficulty, for there are certain areas in England and Wales which, by common consent, would be the choice of the whole nation. The Lake District, 'Snowdonia' and the North Wales mountains, the Peak District with Dovedale, the North Yorkshire coast and moors, the Pembroke coast, the Cornish coast, Exmoor and Dartmoor—surely everybody would agree that these places should be made secure for all time from destruction, if such be possible, safe from the despoiler whether he be a private person or a department of State, preserved and protected for ever.

And let it be repeated once more that this preservation of selected areas does not mean that the smaller areas can be forgotten or in any way neglected. It is equally important that the smaller areas of attractive landscape, such as the Malverns, the Cotswolds, the Mendips, the Quantocks, which may be thought to be unsuitable for national action, but which have the strongest possible local appeal, should also be protected and preserved. National parks are national possessions, created by the nation for the use of the whole nation. The functions of local government as they affect the citizen's personal life will be quite unaffected, but the control of land use will be in national hands, making use no doubt of local knowledge and experience in the fullest and most cordial way. Preservation of natural beauty is therefore of the first importance.

But national parks are not merely a work of preservation; they have a most important positive side. They are not to be thought of only as places of great natural beauty set aside in their integrity, and to be revered and admired from afar; they are to be used in the best possible way to the advantage of the people. They are to be dedicated in truth to the public service. To this end, the national park areas are to be protected as a whole. For example, the Lake District covers an area of 800 square miles, and it is intended that the whole of it shall be protected and preserved—not only the high and solitary places, the majesty of Scawfell, the lonely fells with the wandering tracks going up to the high stone walls, but Borrowdale also and the Langdale Valley and Grasmere and Rydal, the hamlets and the villages, the little towns, the local traditions, the ways of life and livelihood, indeed everything which makes the Lake District the incomparable thing it is.

This wider aspect of preservation has an interesting history, and before dealing shortly with the way national parks are to be used, it might be proper to interpose a word on that history and to state the grounds for the high expectation that national parks will shortly come into being.

The first and greatest name in the history of national parks is that of Wordsworth. J. K. Stephen, in one of the greatest of parodies, pointed out that Wordsworth had two voices, as Swinburne and Rossetti did in rather a different way. But Wordsworth himself thought that he had the qualities for three vocations, those of the poet, the landscape gardener, and the art critic. To the poet our debt is unpayable, but Wordsworth has put us still further into his debt by the publication of that remarkable book—*A Guide to the Lakes.* Although it is now some 135 years old, it is much more than an ancient Guide Book; it is in truth the first Handbook to national parks. Wordsworth desired to save the Lake District from injury at a time when 'the feeling for the rugged and mysterious in nature had become a fashionable affectation', and when ignorant hands were likely to destroy the tranquil, the lovely, and the perfect. The Guide might very well be in the hands of every supporter of national parks, not only for its superlative knowledge and understanding of natural beauty and its significance, not only for the practical wisdom displayed on every page, and down to the smallest detail, but for the statement of purpose which may well stand for the purpose of the larger scene:

> The author has been induced to speak thus at length by a wish to preserve the native beauty of this delightful district....In this wish, the author will be joined by persons of pure taste throughout the whole island, who by their visits (often repeated) to the Lakes in the North of England, testify that they deem the district a sort of national property, in which every man has a right and interest who has an eye to perceive and a heart to enjoy.

Wordsworth has had many successors in purpose, but in greatness he stands alone. In the main, his work has been carried on by the great voluntary societies.

The Commons, Open Spaces and Footpaths Preservation Society was established in 1865, the National Trust in 1895, the Council for the Preservation of Rural England in 1926, and to these have been added from time to time all those organizations which further the interests of walkers, climbers, cyclists, motorists, campers, holiday makers, and all lovers of the open air.

Since the year 1909 powers for the planning and control of land have been in existence, but until April of 1933 statutory planning was largely confined to areas adjoining urban centres of population. The Town and Country Planning Act of 1932 upon which such high hopes were founded has proved a great disappointment. The powers were inadequate to provide national parks even had they been employed to the full, and this situation remains despite the increased powers given by the Acts of 1943 and 1944. Indeed, after twenty years of planning powers the Government of the day in 1929 appointed a strong Committee to consider and report if it is desirable and feasible to establish one or more national parks in Great Britain. This was a most notable step forward, and the Committee received evidence from every quarter. They issued their *Report* in 1931 urging the creation of national parks, and concluded with these words:

> We desire to record our conviction that such measures as we have advocated are necessary if the present generation is to escape the charge that in a short-sighted pursuit of its immediate ends it has squandered a noble heritage.

Fourteen years have passed since those words were published, and for ten of those years, the Friends of the Lake District and the Standing Committee on National Parks, to name the two bodies with which I am connected, have fought many battles to prevent the heritage being squandered. It is this experience, no doubt, which gives me some understanding of the Old Testament prophets, two of whom have now edged their way into this Lecture, though Joel himself could not now restore the years that the locust hath eaten, to say nothing of the cankerworm and the caterpillar and the palmerworm.

But events are now moving swiftly. Three years ago, the Committee presided over by Lord Justice Scott presented a comprehensive and valuable report recommending the creation of national parks as 'certain large areas in the country which are of exceptional natural beauty and scenic interest which should be preserved for the enjoyment of the whole nation'. This is almost the language of Wordsworth in 1810.

In the White Paper on Control of Land Use presented to Parliament by the Minister of Town and Country Planning, one of the aims there set forth is 'the preservation of land for national parks', and though this is not a declaration of Government policy, there can be no doubt after the declarations of Ministers beginning with Lord Portal as Minister of Works and Planning in 1942 that national parks are a part of government policy. The present Minister, Mr W. S. Morrison, has repeatedly expressed his approval of national parks, and under his direction a detailed survey has been made of some of the areas which are thought to be suitable, and which one day will certainly be national parks. The *Report* containing this survey will be published almost immediately, and is bound to be a document of the highest importance, for the many problems connected with national parks will be exhaustively discussed, and authoritatively expounded. The essential details, absent from this Lecture, will be found in all their fullness there.

National parks are therefore most clearly on the way, and it is fitting that at this particular moment in our history they should be established.

But national parks are not to be thought of as museum

pieces; they are to be used, and brought into full public service.

In all the national parks, therefore, a flourishing agriculture will be encouraged. Improved hill-grazings—with better inside pasture and meadow, with better housing and comfort—are obvious needs of agriculture. National parks and agriculture will most assuredly be the best of friends. And indeed they have good cause to be so, for use and beauty, here, at least, go hand in hand. The beauties of the countryside are due in large measure to the fact that the land has been continuously farmed; and it must continue to be farmed if those features which give it distinctive charm and character are not to be lost. Indeed, were there no other reasons for maintaining agriculture in a high state of efficiency after the war, this great reason would still hold good: that it is the only way to preserve the countryside in the traditional aspect known and loved by many generations of men. The landscape of England is most usually described as an attractive patchwork, and the brown ploughlands and the green pastures, the wayward hedges and the winding lanes, the woodlands, the streams, the moorland and downs fully justify the name. The work of nature and the work of man are most happily blended, but if the hand of man were taken quite away, the landscape would go back to forest and scrub, to thorn and bracken.

In that remarkable and suggestive book—*The Changing Face of England*—Anthony Collett wrote:

Few scenes in England are either what Nature first made them or the product of the single purpose of man.

They bear the stamp of two or three thousand years of almost continuous modelling: the architecture of the fields and hills is of as many periods as that of the churches they embosom.

And Mr H. E. Bates, whose writings on the countryside have given so much pleasure, and whose versatility is so much admired, says in that book called *O More than Happy Countryman*:

We make a great struggle, and rightly so, to preserve acres of downland and moor and woodland and forest from the dangers of so-called progress. We rightly estimate that it would be a catastrophe if the English countryside were bit by bit robbed of such features. But if the day ever comes when the English farms can no longer afford to grow oats and barley, wheat and potatoes, to lay fields for hay, to graze cattle and herd sheep, then we shall be faced with a still deeper catastrophe, and the loss of a kind of beauty which we take as naturally for granted as the air we breathe.

The Ministry of Agriculture with all the experience of the war years will no doubt desire to see a healthy and prosperous agriculture everywhere, and the National Park Commissioners will co-operate with the Ministry of Agriculture and with the farmers to maintain the highest standards, for the preservation of the landscape and the needs of agriculture are inextricably intertwined.

But there is yet something more. National parks are to be preserved in their natural beauty, and they are to be continued and stimulated in their farming use; but they are also to be made accessible (in so far as they are not cultivated) for open-air recreation and public enjoyment, and most particularly for cross-country walking.

We are the most urban nation in the world. The 41 million people of England and Wales are spread out on each square mile of the land to the number of 703, compared with the 197 of France or the 43 of America. More than one-third of the population of England and Wales lives in London, Birmingham, Manchester, Liverpool, Leeds, Bradford and the Tyneside. More than half the population lives in or near the fourteen chief urban centres. Thus it comes about that many of the most devout lovers of the countryside are compelled by a harsh and inexorable fate to live in towns, 'banished to the cities not without deleterious effects on imagination, inspiration, and creative power', to quote the Master of Trinity once more. In the last thirty years there has been a considerable flight from the towns into the country, and during the war, of course, for whole populations the country has been a refuge indeed. The motor car has changed the ways of life in the most radical fashion, and has given the most powerful encouragement to the growing desire to see more of the countryside; and nothing is more certain than that the years immediately ahead are going to see that desire manifested on an immense scale.

It is this state of affairs that has produced a great and sometimes a violent conflict of ideas. There are those who would try to keep the country from the town, and those who would try to keep the town from the country. There are those who would try to save the countryside by a revival of the ancient crafts, and the restoration of an attractive world that is, for the moment, gone. There are those, too, who think that town and country are not separate and opposing things to be kept resolutely apart, but that they are bound together by cords which cannot be broken, the one rightly and beneficially complementary to the other. In whatever way that conflict is ultimately resolved, this one thing is certain: there never was a time when the desire on the part of great multitudes of people to reach and enjoy the country was stronger, and there never was a time when the right use of the countryside was more important to the nation. That being so, nothing but good can come from these selected national park areas being preserved and protected by the nation, and being made accessible for public use.

It would be an ill service to deny the danger to complete preservation which lies in easy accessibility. There is great force and truth in the saying—'The tripper is a dangerous denizen of any sanctuary'. But the danger must be faced, and access to the national parks and full facilities for open-air enjoyment must be provided, if national parks are to fulfil their true mission. National parks are for those who wish to enjoy beauty and are content to find their enjoyment in ways that do not injure it. There are millions in that category, and the dangerous denizens need not be unduly feared. One of those millions was portrayed by Mr Wells in 'Mr Polly', the young man tied to the town, and the shop, and the counter, whose soul was athirst for the beauty of the countryside; and for myself, whenever I am tempted to dwell too much on the danger of those who would be happier elsewhere, I return again and again to that moment, when the long morning of cross-country walking accomplished, the happiness of Mr Polly is at its height:

> The glorious moment of standing lordly in the Inn doorway, and staring out at the world, the swinging sign, the geese upon the green, the duck pond, a waiting wagon, the church tower, a sleepy cat, the blue heavéns, and the sizzle of the frying bacon behind one.

To give pleasure like that to millions far outweighs the danger which comes from the few; and of the few this can be said with confidence, that if the likings and preferences are for those pleasures which are to be found in the towns and the popular resorts (and there are such), the darkened Picture House, the lighted Dance Hall, the proximity of crowds—their visits to national parks will not be many, and in time all danger will be past. Even Charles Lamb, writing to Wordsworth, said that 'separate from the pleasure of your company, I don't much care if I never see a mountain in my life', and went on to express a preference for the lighted shops of the Strand and Fleet Street, and even the bustle and wickedness round about Covent Garden. The grounds of complaint which country folk have against some of the visitors from the town will vanish as the standard of good manners becomes universal, and the spread of Education will do much to that end. But adequate holiday facilities will have to be provided, particularly for campers and walkers. Hotels, hostels, camp sites, car-parks, shelters, farm buildings, village halls, sign posts for public footpaths—all these will require the careful attention of the National Park Commissioners, and formidable and indeed frightening as the bare list sounds when read, all these things can be done with taste and discretion, so that the peace of the countryside is not offended.

And now that I may bind up these scattered sayings with the whole, let me end as I began, by saying that there is no obstacle to national parks at this time which cannot quite easily be overcome.

National parks can quite easily fit into the existing pattern of land ownership, and public acquisition is in no sense essential. Questions of compensation do not present serious difficulties in national park areas, but it is important that they should be dealt with and overcome before the parks are set up. National parks, by their very nature, are in undeveloped country for the most part, and are free from those building values which are created by the close proximity of towns; and the settlement of the question of compensation is essential to that firm financial basis on which the special protection of national parks must be built.

Even quite embittered questions, such as the right of ramblers in the national park areas to walk over grouse moors or water-catchment areas, are capable of solution; and it must be enough here to repeat that national parks can be brought into being at once, with no real disturbance of the national life, and with immeasurable benefit to the people.

It is not given to everybody to know how great that benefit can be, but perhaps it would not be unfitting to end this Lecture with the words of one who did, and was able to give his understanding immortal expression:

> Once again I see
> These hedge-rows, hardly hedge-rows, little lines
> Of sportive wood run wild: these pastoral farms,
> Green to the very door; and wreaths of smoke
> Sent up, in silence, from among the trees!
> These beauteous forms,
> Through a long absence, have not been to me
> As is a landscape to a blind man's eye;
> But oft, in lonely rooms, and 'mid the din
> Of towns and cities, I have owed to them,
> In hours of weariness, sensations sweet,
> Felt in the blood, and felt along the heart!
> And passing even into my purer mind,
> With tranquil restoration: feelings too
> Of unremembered pleasure: such, perhaps,
> As have no slight or trivial influence
> On that best portion of a good man's life,
> His little, nameless, unremembered acts
> Of kindness and of love. Nor less, I trust,
> To them I may have owed another gift,
> Of aspect more sublime; that blessed mood,
> In which the burthen of the mystery,

In which the heavy and the weary weight
Of all this unintelligible world,
Is lightened: that serene and blessed mood,
In which the affections gently lead us on,
Until, the breath of this corporeal frame
And even the motion of our human blood
Almost suspended, we are laid asleep
In body, and become a living soul:
While with an eye made quiet by the power
Of harmony, and the deep power of joy,
We see into the life of things.

Lightning Source UK Ltd.
Milton Keynes UK
UKHW041826160321
380430UK00007B/158

9 781107 674776